JN408978

# 바다에서 별을 낚다

I Fished Up a Star from the Sea

류인순 한영시집
Ryu In-Soon's Korean-English Poetry Collection

# 바다에서 별을 낚다

## I Fished Up a Star from the Sea

시 | 류인순 Written by Ryu In-Soon
번역 | 류인순 Translated by Ryu In-Soon

도서출판 천우

## 시인의 말

**하늘 멋진 날**
**오늘은 사랑하기 좋은 날**
**그대를 마음껏 사랑하고 싶은 날**

문학 활동 시작한 후 20년이 지난 지금 나의 첫 번째 한영시집『바다에서 별을 낚다』를 선보인다. 이 시집은 한국어와 영어로 번역된 작품들이 수록되어 있으며 독자가 원문과 번역문을 동시에 읽을 수 있도록 한 권의 책 안에 두 언어를 나란히 배치하였고 각 부마다 자연의 아름답고 섬세한 변화를 통해 우리 삶의 여러 측면을 탐구하고 삶의 본질적인 사랑, 이별, 그리움, 희망을 담아냈다.

한영시집을 출간하게 된 계기는 2024년도 류인순 제2시집『담쟁이 붉게 익었다』시집 발간 후 해당 시집을 해외 몇 곳에 150부 이상 기증한 것을 계기로, 한글로만 된 시가 외국인에게 의미 전달이 제대로 될까 하는 아쉬움이 있었고 다른 언어를 사용하는 독자들도 번역을 통해 이 시집에 담긴 감정을 공유할 수 있기를 바라는 마음에서이다.

이 시집이 다른 언어를 사용하는 외국인에게도 단순한 언어의 나열이 아닌 마음과 마음을 잇는 다리 역할이

되었으면 하는 바람과 함께 이 시집을 통해 더 많은 독자와 소통하고 그들의 마음에 닿기를 소망한다.

오늘도 문학인으로 산다는 자부심으로 언제나 변함없을 내 삶에 친구이자 연인, 특히 자연의 아름다움을 곱게 빚어 한 권의 책으로 엮어 나의 한영시집 『**바다에서 별을 낚다**』를 설렘으로 세상에 내민다.

2025년 여름, 달빛 내리는 작업실에서

가향 류인순

## The Poet's Words

**A Beautiful Day in the Sky**
**Today is a perfect day to love**
**A day I want to love you with all my heart**

Twenty years after beginning my literary career, I now present my first Korean-English poetry collection, 『I Fished Up a Star from the Sea』. This collection of poetry contains works translated into Korean and English, and the two languages are placed side by side in one book so that readers can read the original and translated texts at the same time. Each part explores various aspects of our lives through the beautiful and delicate changes in nature and captures the essential love, separation, longing, and hope of life.

The reason for publishing this Korean-English poetry collection stems from the experience of donating over 150 copies of Ryu In Soon's second poetry collection, 『The Ivy Has Ripened Red』, to several locations abroad after its release in 2024. During this process, a sense of regret arose about whether poems written solely in Korean could effectively convey their meaning to foreign readers. The hope is that readers who speak other languages can also share in the emotions embedded in this poetry collection through translation.

I hope that this collection of poems will serve as a bridge between hearts and minds, rather than just a list of words, for foreigners who speak other languages, and I hope to communicate with more readers and reach their hearts through this collection of poems.

With the pride of living as a literary person, I beautifully shape the unchanging beauty of friends, lovers, and especially nature into my life, weaving them into a single book, and with excitement, I present my Korean-English poetry collection, 『**I Fished Up a Star from the Sea**』 to the world.

In the summer of 2025,
in the study where the moonlight falls.
Poet Ryu In Soon

# 음유시인 류인순 작가의 한영시집 발간에 부쳐

## On the Publication of Minstrel Poet Ryu In-Soon's Korean-English Poetry Collection

감성철학자 김 천 우
(사)세계문인협회 이사장 · 문학평론가

Emotional Philosopher Chunwoo Kim
President of the World Writers Association & Literary Critic

음유시인 류인순 작가의 제 3시집 상재『바다에서 별을 낚다』(I Fished Up a Star from the Sea)는 시인의 제2시집『담쟁이 붉게 익었다』뜨거운 선풍 이후 주옥같은 작품세계로 발간하는 한영시집으로서 독자들의 기대 또한 대단히 크다고 본다. 저자 본인이 직접 번역을 하는 터라 시의 주제와 깊은 뜻이 함축되어 있으며 원문과 번역문을 동시에 읽을 수 있도록 배려하는 저자의 깔끔하고 담백한 시인정신이 참으로 고귀하고 섬세하다고 본다.

음유시인 류인순 작가는 시인으로, 노랫말을 짓는 작사가로 디지털 시대를 접목한 현대시의 중심부인 디카시 부문으로 공식 등단 입문한 중견작가로 자리매김하고 있다. (사)세계문인협회 이사 직분을 중심으로 시 낭송가의 열정을 불사르는 모습이 점점 더 진정성 있는 참모습을 보여주고 있는 한영시집은 노벨문학상 쾌거를 낳은 한강 작가의 열기가 한몫하지 않았나 하는 생각도 들 만큼『바다에서 별을 낚다』시세계는 등단 입문

20여 년 동안 언어의 연금술을 녹여낸 수작이라 할 만큼 탄탄하다. 제1부 마법 같은 커피, 제2부 바람 지나는 길 하나 내자, 제3부 안탈리아 해변에서, 제4부 호수에 걸린 낮달, 제5부 가을 숲에 서면, 제6부 그래 봄이야로 나누어져 있다.

각부마다 독특하고 신선함을 부여해 주는 시적 화자는 흠잡을 데 없이 깔끔한 단락으로 구성되어 있으며 여류작가로서 보기 드문 실력을 골고루 갖춘 소신 있는 작가임에는 틀림이 없다. 독일의 저명한 헤르만 헤세의 작품 세계관과, 프랑스 장 폴, 사르트르, 실존주의 철학사상 속, 문학적 배경은 헤겔과 니체, 키르케고르 등의 영향도 받은 듯 류인순 시인의 음유적인 포괄성도 자유로운 영혼으로 스스로 고독의 성벽을 넘어선 목표 설정과 창작 정신은 끊임없는 열정과 자아 성찰을 통하여 자신을 누구보다 사랑하는 면면들의 시의 화자들을 통하여 역력히 드러나 있다. 시는 그 사람의 자화상이다. 시인의 제 3시집을 통찰해 보니 레오 버스카글리아의 "사랑은 상대를 있는 그대로 받아들이는 것이다"라는 구절과 진정한 사랑은 서로를 마주 보는 것이 아니라, 같은 방향을 바라보는 것이라는 생텍쥐페리의 글귀가 클로즈업되는 것은 음유시인 류인순의 작품집에도 투영되는 그 진가가 빛으로 발산하는 듯 한영시집 발간을 계기로 노벨문학상 도전도 가능하지 않을까? 하는 욕심을 부려보고 싶은 걸쭉한 작품이라고 본다.

# 제1부 마법 같은 커피
# Part I Magical Coffee

## 제2부 바람 지나는 길 하나 내자

## Part II Let's Create a Path for the Wind to Pass Through

# 제3부 안탈리아 해변에서
# Part III On the Beaches of Antalya

## 제4부 호수에 걸린 낮달
## Part IV A Daytime Moon Hanging Over the Lake

## 제5부 가을 숲에 서면
## Part V When I Stand in the Autumn Forest

# 제6부 그래 봄이야
## Part VI So, It's Spring

# 제 1 부

# 마법 같은 커피

## Part Ⅰ

## Magical Coffee

# 마법 같은 커피

머그잔 속 맴도는
쌉싸래한 커피 향기
오늘은 입안 가득
달콤한 노래가 됩니다

쓴맛마저도 달콤하게
마법 같은 커피는
내 안에
숨겨 둔 은밀한 사랑

입술 끝에 남은 떨림
말하지 못한 고백
한 모금마다
그대라는 이름입니다.

## Magical Coffee

Hovering in a mug
A bitter smell of coffee
My mouth is full today
It becomes a sweet song

Even the bitter taste is sweet
Coffee is like magic
Inside me
Hidden secret love

A tremor left at the end of the lips
Unsaid confession
At every sip
It's the name that is you.

# 빈 의자

내 마음 정원에
빈 의자 하나
마련해 두었습니다

삶의 간이역에
특별히 마련한
영혼 맑히는 안식처

힘겨운 여정 속
그대 쉼 필요할 때
언제든지 오세요

빈 의자 하나
오직 그대만을 위한
나의 선물입니다.

## Empty Chair

In the garden of my heart
One empty chair
I have prepared it

At the midpoint of life way station
Specially prepared
A sanctuary to purify the soul

In a difficult journey
When you need rest
Come anytime

One empty chair
Only for you
This is a gift I prepared.

# 등대지기

밤바다 별 사이에서
어민들 인도하는 나침반
바다 위의 수호신으로
희망의 불씨 던져준다

휘청거리는 세상에서도
흔들림 하나 없이
묵묵히 자리 지키며
홀로 고독을 삼키고

깊은 밤 거센 파도가
쉴 새 없이 포말 토해도
바다의 맥박처럼
고요히 숨 쉬고 있다

그대에게도
삶에 등불 밝혀 주는
영혼의 나침반
등대지기 하나 있는가.

## Lighthouse Keeper

Between the stars in the night sea
A compass that guides fishermen
As a guardian on the sea
Gives a spark of hope

Even in a reeling world
Without any shaking
Staying silently
Swallowing solitude alone

The strong waves in the deep night
Even if I vomit foam non-stop
Like the pulse of the sea
Breathe in silence

To you too
A beacon to life
Soul compass
Is there a lighthouse keeper.

# 차를 마시며

까닭 없이 외로울 때
생각나는 사람이 있다

마음속에 담으면
한 잔의 차가 되는 사람

닿을 듯 닿지 않는
그대와 나 사이

먼 훗날 그날엔
우리 만날 수 있을까.

# Thinking Over a Cup of Tea

When you feel lonely for no reason
There is someone that comes to mind

If you keep it in your heart
A person who becomes a cup of tea

It seems like it can be reached but it can't be reached
Between you and me

On that day in the distant future
Will can you and I meet.

## 숲에 두고 온 비밀

가을 설악산 중턱
울산바위 가는 길
숲에서 만난 돌탑 하나

하나둘 그 누군가
비밀스러운 소망
아슬아슬 쌓아 놓았네

인생길 길목마다
수 없이 낚은 욕심
비우고자 떠난 그날

켜켜이 쌓은 소망
묵직한 돌탑 위로
또 다른 소망 올라가고

툭툭 비워 낸 자리
아뿔싸,
욕심 하나 또 담았네

비밀스러운 나의
작지만 큰
그 무엇보다 간절한.

## The Secret I Left in the Forest

Mid-slope of Mt. Seoraksan in autumn
On the way to Ulsanbawi
A stone tower I found in the forest

One by one, someone
Secret wishes
Carefully and precariously stacked

Everywhere in life
The many desires fished
The day I left to empty them

Layered wishes
Upon the heavy stone tower
Another wish climbs up

Lightly emptied space
Oh my,
I added another desire

My own secret
Small but great
Most earnest than anything else.

# 내 마음 오선지

마음 맑아 좋은 날엔
한 옥타브 높게 그려
푸른 하늘 날아보고

마음 흐려 힘든 날엔
한 옥타브 낮게 그려
쉼표 하나 찍어 본다

아름다운 선율 속에
숨겨진 엇박자는
화음으로 조율하고

도돌이표 없는 인생길
이왕이면 오늘도
고운 음표 그려 넣자.

## The Staff Within My Heart

On a good day when my heart is clear
Drawing one octave higher
Let's fly in the blue sky

On difficult days when my heart becomes clouded
Drawing one octave lower
Will try to put a comma

In a beautiful melody
The hidden offbeat is
Will tune to harmony

A path in life that cannot be returned
If possible today too
Let's draw some beautiful notes.

# 내 니 올 줄 알았다

갈바람 불면
가슴팍 숭숭
바람 소리 난다고 했지

텅 빈 가슴
진한 에스프레소 한 잔에도
마음 말랑해지는 곳

상처 난 옹이에
단풍 다붓이 내려앉아
살살 어루만져 주고

솔바람 청아한 노래에
구름도 쉬어 가고
바람도 머물다 가는 곳

오색 물결 춤추는
가을 숲속 카페에
내 니 올 줄 알았다.

# I Knew You'd Come

When the autumn breeze blows
Empty heart
You said it sounded like the wind

Empty chest
Even with a cup of strong espresso
A place where one's heart becomes soft

On the wounded stump
The autumn leaves fall down
It is caressing gently

In the clear song of the pine breeze
Even the clouds rest and pass by
A place where the wind stays and passes by

Five-colored wavy dancing
This cafe in the autumn forest
I knew you'd come.

# 흔들릴 때가 있다

항해하다 보면
배가 풍랑에
심하게 흔들릴 때가 있다

배가 흔들리는 것도
항해의 일부이듯

내가 흔들리는 것도
삶의 일부이고
살아 있다는 증거다

아무리 센바람도
언젠가는 잦아들 테니
꽃씨 하나 다시 심자.

## There are Times When Life Gets Shaken

While sailing
The ship can be caught in the storm
There are moments of intense shaking

The boat shaking as well
Part of the sailing

My shaking is also
A part of life
It's proof that I'm alive

No matter how strong the wind is
One day, it's gonna die down
So I will plant flower seeds again.

## 자귀나무꽃

분홍빛 선녀 옷자락인가
수백 마리 나비인가
그도 아니면 곱게 펼친 부채인가

눈길 사로잡는 그 모습에
가던 길 멈추고
임 보듯 너를 본다

여름날 자귀나무꽃
내 가슴에도
그리움 한 자락 꽃 피고

한 송이 따서 볼에 비비면
임 생각할 때처럼
내 볼이 발그레 물들 것 같다.

## The Silk Tree Flower

Is it the pink hem of a fairy's dress
Are there hundreds of butterflies
Or is it a neatly opened fan

It caught my eye
I stopped on my way
I see you the way I see someone I love

Silk tree flowers on a summer day
Even in my heart
A flower of longing blooms

If you pick one and rub it on your cheek
Like when I think about the person I love
My cheeks are going to turn red.

# 꽃샘추위

달달한 아침 햇살에
봄인가 하고
속적삼 바람으로
빼꼼히 문 열어보니

어이쿠 깜짝이야
엎드려 숨어 있던 겨울
벌떡 일어서서
와락 목덜미 걸머잡네

해마다 너의 심통에
몸살감기 앓았는데
아뿔싸,
올해 또 당했네.

# The Cold that Envies the Spring Flowers

In the sweet morning sunlight
I thought it was spring
Wear light clothes
I opened the door carefully

Oh, I was surprised
The winter that lay low and hid
Suddenly got up
Grabbed me by the scruff

Because of your grumpiness every year
I had body ache and a cold
Oh my god,
I got it again this year.

제 2 부

# 바람 지나는 길 하나 내자

Part Ⅱ

# Let's Create a Path for the Wind to Pass Through

# 나도 한번 해 볼 걸

해외 여행길에 올라
호텔 카운터 앞
외국어 실력 총동원해
소통하고 한숨 돌리는데

뒤따라 들어온 그녀
호텔 카운터를 향한
거침없는 목소리
대뜸 한국어가 춤을 추네

당당한 그녀 앞에
호텔 직원도
한국어로 속닥속닥
일사천리 상황 종료

아뿔싸!
나도 한번 해 볼 걸
우리말이 통할는지
우선 한번 해 볼걸

세계 속에 한국어
드높이 날개 달고
만국 공통어 될 그날
손꼽아 기다려보네.

# I Should Have Tried It Too

Go on a trip abroad
In front of the hotel counter
Mobilize all your foreign language skills
We communicate and take a breather

She came in after me
Towards the hotel counter
An outspoken voice
Suddenly Korean starts dancing

Having the confident her in front
Hotel staff too
Whispering in Korean
Ending the situation in a flash

Oh my!
I should have tried it too
Will our language communicate
I should have tried it once

Korean in the world
With wings soaring high
The day that will become a universal language
I eagerly await the day.

# 바다에서 별을 낚다

이 세상 소풍 나와
지나는 길목마다
낚싯대 길게 뻗어
수 없이 낚은 욕심

바닷가 백사장에 앉아
낚싯줄도 미끼도 없이
빈 낚싯대 드리우고
쉼표 하나 찍으며

걸머쥔 욕심 풀어
깊은 바다 수평선 너머
하나둘 날려 보내
툭툭 비워 낸 자리

대낮에도 눈 부시는
별 하나 건져 담으니
아,
이게 바로 천국이구나.

# I Fished Up a Star from the Sea

Having come out for a picnic in this world
Along every path I travel
Casting my fishing rod far and wide
Caught a multitude of desires

Sitting on the sandy beach by the sea
With neither a line nor bait
After casting an empty fishing rod
Pausing with a comma

Let go of the desires that were being clutched
Beyond the deep sea horizon
One by one, send them flying
The space left empty with light taps

It shines brightly even in the daytime
Reeled in a star and raised it
Ah,
It is truly heaven.

## 바람 지나는 길 하나 내자

살다가 만난 수많은 인연
곁에 머물 인연은
붙잡지 않아도 머물고
스쳐 갈 인연은
붙잡아도 바람처럼 사라지니
내 마음에
바람 지나는 길 하나 내자

세월은 지금도 달음박질 중이다
걸어온 길 돌아보지 말고
걸어갈 길 아름답게 꾸며보자
우리네 백 세 인생이라지만
먹고 자고 놀고 나면
이 세상 소풍 길에
꽃 피울 시간 그리 길지 않다

비움이 없으면 채움도 없으니
묵은 것 툭툭 비워내고
하나둘 새로운 것 채우면서
바람처럼 흩어질 인연은

미련 없이 지나가도록
내 마음에
바람 지나는 길 하나 내자.

## Let's Create a Path for the Wind to Pass Through

The many relationships I have met in my life
The fate that will stay by my side
Stay even if I don't hold on
The fate that will pass by
Even if I hold on to it, it disappears like the wind
In my heart
Let's create a path for the wind to pass through

Time is still running fast
Don't look back on the path took
Let's make the path walk ahead beautiful
Even if we live for 100 years
After eating, sleeping and playing
On a picnic in this world
The flowering time is shorter than you think

If there is no emptying, there is no filling
Empty out the old stuff
Filling in new things one by one
A relationship that will scatter like the wind

So that it passes without regrets

In my heart

Let's create a path for the wind to pass through.

## 담쟁이 붉게 익었다

봄날 희망 하나 안고
가파른 담벼락
밤낮 쉼 없이 오르네

삶의 길
고지를 향해 묵묵히
오르고 또 오르네

한여름
뜨거운 열기 세찬 폭우
악착스레 견뎌내고

이 가을
붉게 익은 그 모습에
뜨거워지는 내 심장.

## The Ivy Has Ripened Red

With one hope on a spring day
Steep wall
It rises without rest day and night

The path of life
Silently towards the highlands
It goes up and up again

Midsummer
Hot heat and heavy rain
Stubbornly endured it

This Autumn
Looking at that red ripe sight
My heart is getting hotter.

# 연리지

해 뜨고 달 뜨고
천년 바람 속에서도
묵묵히 자리 지키며

뼛속까지 시려오는
혼자라는 외로움에
곁눈질로 익은 사랑

손 내밀어 닿는 곳
밤낮으로 곁에 서서
서로 상처 보듬으며

간절한 마음 맞닿아
뗄 수 없는 운명으로
하나가 된 사랑이여.

# Yeonriji

The sun rises and the moon rises
In the midst of a thousand years of wind
Keep one's seat quietly

Cold to the bone
In the loneliness of being alone
Love that is ripe with a sideways glance

A place within reach of
Standing together day and night
We are taking care of each other's wounds

Our earnest hearts touched each other
With an inseparable fate
It's love that became one.

# 기차에 추억 싣고

십수 년 만에 기차에 올라
창밖에 시선을 두니
잊힌 줄 알았던 추억 하나
대롱대롱 매달린다

어린아이 때 처음 탄 기차
창밖 풍경이 뒤로 달아나며
순간이동 하는 듯 신기해서
눈과 입이 마구 들떠 있었지

내 살아온 뒤안길엔
어떤 풍경이 사라지고
난 무엇을 남기고 왔을까
문득 깊은 생각에 잠긴다

사계절 아름다운 풍경처럼
내가 걸어온 풍경에도
아름다운 흔적이
총총 남았으면 참 좋겠다.

# Memories on the Train

Boarding a train for the first time in ten years
When I looked out the window
A memory I thought had been forgotten
Hanging languidly

The first train as a child
The view outside the window ran back
It was incredibly fascinating, like I was teleporting
My eyes and mouth were so excited

In the back of my life
I wonder what kind of scenery has vanished
What did I leave behind
Suddenly I fall into deep thought

Like beautiful scenery in all four seasons
Even in the scenery that I walked
Beautiful traces
I really wish there were more left.

## 마음 뺄셈

세월 따라
얽히고설킨
수많은 인연의 고리

나이 더 할수록
버거운 인연들을
서서히 털어낸다

마음이 가벼워야
몸도 가볍고
건강하게 사는 길

마음 곳간에서
하나둘 뺄셈하고
더 가볍게 가볍게

내가 온전히
감당할 수 있을 만큼
딱 그만큼만.

## Subtraction by Heart

As the years pass
Intertwined
A ring of many ties

As I get older
Burdensome relationships
Shake off gradually

If mind is light
The body is also light
The way to live in health

In the storehouse of my mind
Subtracting one by one
More lightly More lightly

I completely
As much as I can handle
Just as much as.

## 비밀 해제

이건 비밀인데
너한테만 말할 게

아무한테도
절대
말하지 마!

## Secret Unlock

This is a secret
I'll tell you only

To nobody
Never
Don't say it!

# 사월의 봄

벌거벗은 가지마다
연둣빛 새 옷 갈아입고

명주바람 간지럼에
복사꽃 웃음보 터지네

산자락 색칠하는 진달래
잠자던 분홍빛 연정 깨우고

화려한 춤사위로
온 천지 꽃 잔치 열리면

내 가슴에도
그대란 꽃 활짝 피고.

## The Spring in April

Every bare branch
Changed into new light green clothes

In the tickling of the soft wind
The peach blossom smiled brightly

When azaleas color the mountainside
Awakening the sleeping pink love

While dancing splendidly
When flower festivals are held all over the country

In my heart too
The flower called you is starting to bloom.

# 비 오는 날이면

잊은 줄 알았는데
모든 그리움도
사라진 줄 알았는데

비 오는 날이면
너는 내 안에서
조용히 살아나고

지운 줄 알았는데
그리움이 창가에서
몸살을 앓고 있다.

## On Rainy Days

I thought I had forgotten
All the longings
I thought it was gone

On rainy days
You are inside me
Quietly revived

I thought I had erased it
Longing sitting at the window
Suffering from a body ache.

제3부

# 안탈리아 해변에서

Part Ⅲ

# On the Beaches of Antalya

# 안탈리아 해변에서

푸른 바다 지중해 품은
튀르키예 휴양지
안탈리아 알브살라르 해변

여름이 절정에 치닫는 날
해변에 모인 각국 여행객들
모두가 환한 웃음꽃이다

내 안에 길 따라
가만가만 속삭이는
파도 소리는 낭만을 부르는데

해 질 녘 바닷가
수평선에 걸린 석양은
또 하루의 젊음을 삼켜버리고

여름 해변 파도는
천년 후에도 또 그렇게
모래알과 사랑 속삭일 것이다.

## On the Beaches of Antalya

The blue waters embrace the Mediterranean
Turkiye Getaway
Antalya's Alb Salar Beach

At the height of summer
Travelers from all over the world gather on the beach
Everyone is smiling brightly

Along the path inside me
Whispering quietly
The sound of the waves is calling for romance

The beach at sunset
The setting sun on the horizon
Swallows up another day's youth

The summer beach waves
Will do so again in a thousand years
Will whisper love to the grains of sand.

# 첫사랑

오월 라일락꽃 핀 교정
연둣빛 햇살 속에
향기로운 꽃잎 닮아
봄처럼 아름답던 너의 미소

설레는 마음 숨긴 채
나란히 걷던 그 길에서
떨리던 너의 숨결
영원처럼 내 가슴에 새겼다

지금은 멀어진 기억의 자리
너는 떠나고 없어도
첫사랑의 자리엔
너라는 봄이 아련히 남아 있다

돌고 돌아 다시 봄날
오월 라일락꽃 필 때면
너의 향기 너의 눈동자
여전히 내 안에 살아 있다.

## First Love

May lilac flower blooming campus
In the light green sunshine
Resemble fragrant petal
Your smile was as beautiful as spring

Hiding my excited heart
On the road we walked side by side
Your trembling breath
Engraved in my heart like eternity

A place of distant memories now
Even though you're gone
In the place of my first love
The spring of you remains nostalgic

Around and around, spring day returns
When the lilacs bloom in May
Your scent Your eyes
It still lives inside me.

## 마음 수리공

무심히 길을 걷다
문득 혼자라고 느낄 때
가슴속 찬 바람 불지만

이 순간도
세상은 나를 중심으로
쉼 없이 돌고 있음에

내 영혼 뜰 안에
꽃씨 하나 다시 심고
새봄 기다리며

내가 나를 사랑하고
내가 내 마음 데운다.

## Heart Repairperson

Walk down the street carelessly
When you suddenly feel alone
Although it's a cold wind in my heart

Even at this moment
The world revolves around me
It keeps spinning endlessly

That's why in the yard of my soul
Plant a flower seed again
Waiting for new spring

I love myself
I warm my heart by myself.

# 사랑하려거든

고슴도치같이 사랑하라
서로 소유하려 들지 말고
너무 가까이 가려 하지 말고
욕심에 가시털 세우지 말고
서로 찔려 상처 생기지 않게
한 발짝 물러나 바라보며
가슴으로 사랑하라

영원한 평행선으로
쉬어가는 간이역에 앉아
함께 숨 고르며
손잡으면 닿을 수 있는
그만큼의 거리에서

바라보는 눈빛만으로
주고받는 속삭임만으로
서로의 온기를 잃지 않는
딱 그만큼의 거리에서.

## If You Wish to Love

Love like a porcupine does
Don't try to own each other
Don't try to get too close
Don't let greed grow a thorn
So that we don't get hurt by stabbing each other
Take a step back and take a look
Love each other in heart

In eternal parallel
Sitting and resting at a small railroad station
Breathe together
If you hold hand you can reach it
At an appropriate distance

Only with the glance to see
Just by exchanging whispers
Enough to not lose each other's warmth
At exactly that interval.

# 친구

차 한잔에 추억 타서 마시며
서로 안부 묻고 무탈함을 알리고
눈빛만으로도 통하는
진실한 친구가 있어서 좋다

시간의 흐름도 잠시 붙들고
학창 시절 별명에도 깔깔웃음으로
한없이 수다 떨어도 흉 될 것 없는
언제나 편안한 사이

살다가, 힘들 때
마주 보는 미소만으로도
서로에게 위안이 되고
손 내밀어 용기를 주는 친구

긴 밤 지새워도 좋을
친구와 수다는 삶의 청량제요
내 영원한 젊음이 거기 살아 있어
세월 흘러도 마음은 청춘인 까닭이다.

## The Friend

Drink with memories in a cup of tea
Ask each other how you're doing and tell each other you're okay
Just by looking into each other's eyes, each other can understand
It's good to have a true friends

Stop the flow of time for a moment
We talked about nicknames and laughed when we were students
There's no problem with talking endlessly
Always on comfortable terms

As you go through life, when tough moments come
Even if we just look at each other with a smile
It's comforting for each other
A friend who reaches out and gives courage

It's okay to talk all night long
Conversations with friend bring vitality to my life
Becouse my eternal youth is there
It is the reason why my heart remains young even as time passes.

# 달팽이 사랑

당신에게 가는 길
서두르지 않으렵니다
그러나 쉬지도 않겠습니다

느릿느릿 갈 수밖에 없지만
내 온몸 혼신을 다해
한 걸음 한 걸음 다가가겠습니다

가다가 지쳐 쓰러져
한 줌의 진토로 변할지라도
당신에게 가는 길 멈추지 않겠습니다

가는 길이 힘들고 험난해도
쉬지 않고 가야 할 까닭은
내 사랑은 오직 당신뿐이니까요.

## Snail Love

The road to you
I won't rush
But I won't rest

I have no choice but to go slowly
But with all my might
I will approach you step by step

After passing out from exhaustion
Even if it becomes a handful of dust
I won't stop on my way to you

Even if the road is difficult and rough
The reason why I have to go without resting
Because my love is only you.

## 주인 없는 모자

호숫가 벤치 위에
주인 없는 모자 하나
햇살 무게를 이고
한여름 견디고 있다

바람이 스칠 때마다
소리 없이 흔들리고
주인 잃은 자리엔
침묵만이 흐르고 있다

어디로 갔을까
함께하던 모자 주인
호수는 대답 없이
잔잔한 물빛만 선물한다

햇살은 모자를 감싸안으며
그 위에 여름을 눕히고
주인 잃은 모자는
그렇게 여름을 살아간다.

## Hat Without an Owner

On the lakeside bench
A hat without an owner
Carrying the weight of sunlight
Enduring the midsummer heat

Every time the wind passes by
Shaking without a sound
In the place where the owner was lost
There is only silence

Where did it go
The owner of a hat that used to be with
The lake doesn't answer
It presents only the calm light of water

The sunlight embraces the hat
Summer was added on top of it
The hat that lost its owner
That's how spends the summer.

# 가을 산에 오르면

솔바람 청아한 선율이
쪽빛 하늘에 빠지고
춤추는 바람결이 곱다

산기슭 돌 틈 사이
오롯이 피어
해맑게 손짓하는 구절초

산등선 억새들
은빛 머릿결 풀어헤쳐
곡예 하듯 춤춘다

붉게 물든 산그늘엔
떠나기 아쉬운 가을이
숨바꼭질하고

솔가지에 놀던 바람은
내 안의 욕심들
사정없이 낚아채 간다.

## When I Climb the Mountain in the Autumn

The fresh melody of the pine breeze
Falls on the indigo sky
The dancing wind is beautiful

Between the stones at the foot of the mountain
It bloomed all alone
Gujeolcho beckons brightly

Silver grass on the mountain ridge
With silver hair loose
Dance like an acrobatic

In the shadow of the ruddy mountains
Autumn that doesn't want to leave
Hide and seek is in full swing

The wind that played on the pine branches
The greed within me
It grabs without hesitation and takes it away.

# 두물머리

남한강 북한강이
천 리 물길 흐르다
혼자는 외로워서
하나로 만났구나

너와 나처럼.

# Dumulmeori

Namhan River and Bukhan River
Having flowed for a great distance
Feeling lonely when alone
Two have become one

Just Like you and me.

## 네잎클로버

공원 산책로
토끼풀밭에 쪼그려 앉아
행운 준다는
네잎클로버 찾는 사람

네 잎은 행운이고
세 잎은 행복이라

온 시선 집중해서
행운 하나 찾겠다고
이리저리 뒤적이네
눈앞에 행복 못 본 채.

## The Four-Leaf Clover

Park trails
Squatting on the rabbit grass field
It is said to bring good luck
A four-leaf clover seeker

Four leaves are lucky
Three leaves are happiness

Focus all attention
Trying to find a piece of luck
Rummaging around
Without seeing happiness in front of one's eyes.

제 4 부

# 호수에 걸린 낮달

Part Ⅳ

# A Daytime Moon Hanging Over the Lake

## 가을 왔다길래

유독 긴 여름 지나
반가운 가을 왔다길래
설렘 안고 나가 보니
색 바랜 옷자락만 보이고

아름다운 너를 만나려
꽃단장했건만
멀어지는 너의 뒷모습
텅 빈 바람만이 흐른다

갈수록 짧아지는 계절
사랑 고백할 틈 없이
색 바랜 낯선 모습으로
멀어지는 너의 발소리

그리움 끝에 만났지만
떠날 채비 한창인 너를
붙잡을 수 없어
씁쓸한 미소만 짓는다.

## I Heard that Autumn Has Come

A particularly long summer has passed
I heard that joyful autumn has come
I went out with excitement
Only the faded hem is visible

To meet the beautiful you
Although it was decorated with flowers
Your back is moving away
Only the empty wind flows

An ever-shorter season
Without a moment to confess one's love
In a faded and unfamiliar way
The sound of your footsteps moving away

I met you after longing
You are preparing to leave
I can't hold you
I'm only smiles bitterly.

# 그대와 커피

아침엔
모닝커피 한 잔

비 오는 날엔
분위기 타서 한 잔

햇살 맑은 날엔
기분 좋아서 한 잔

내가 커피를 좋아하는
수많은 까닭에

나의 일상에 단 하루도
커피를 뗄 수 없네

내 안의 그대처럼.

## Within Me You and Coffee

In the morning
Cup of morning coffee

On rainy days
I'm drinking a cup of coffee in a cozy atmosphere

On a sunny day
I'm drinking a cup of coffee because I feel good

I like coffee
For many reasons

Not a single day in my daily life
I can't quit coffee even

Just like you inside me.

# 오호리 공원 호숫가

지독히도 더웠다
올해 여름
폭염 아직 떠나지 못한
이십사 년 팔 월 끝자락

여름휴가 일탈의 날
망중한 즐기러 찾아간
오호리 공원 호숫가
땡볕과 한판 씨름 중이다

한 발 두 발 거닐다 보니
햇살에 목욕한 수양버들
살랑대는 긴 머리카락
잠자던 추억 하나 깨우고

호숫가 해바라기꽃 사이로
비치는 눈부신 윤슬은
첫사랑 그대 닮아
자꾸만 내 시선 끌어당긴다.

## Ohori Park Lakeside

It was extremely hot
This summer
The heat wave hasn't left yet
At the end of August, the year 2024

Summer vacation escape day
I went there to have fun
Ohori Park lakeside
I'm struggling with the scorching sun

As I walked one step at a time
Weeping willow bathed in sunlight
Long flowing hair
I wake up a sleeping memory

Among the sunflowers by the lakeside
The dazzling light seeping through
First love you resemble
It keeps grabbing my attention.

## 민들레

홀씨로 나풀나풀
바람 무동 타고
양지바른 들판에 내려앉아

야금야금 햇살 먹고
뿌리 깊숙이 내려
노랗게 꽃 피웠다

밤낮으로 그리운
일편단심 그대 생각에
어느새 하얀 머리

저 하늘 훨훨 날아
그대 뜰 안에 내려앉아
다시 꽃 피울 꿈 꾼다.

## Dandelion

Fluttering with a single seed
Riding the wind
Landing on a sunny field

Eat the sunlight little by little
Go down deep roots
Yellow flower has bloomed

Longing day and night
Only thinking of you
My hair was white

Flying high into the sky
Sit down in your yard
I dream of flower blooming again.

## 호수에 걸린 낮달

마장 호수 위에
속살 찌우는 상현달
눈으로 살며시 당겨
겨울나무 빈 가지에
아스라이 올려보고

꿈속의 임 보듯
두 눈에 가득 담아
가지 끝에 매다니
해맑은 임 얼굴 닮은
꽃 한 송이 열리네

넌지시 눈길로 낚아
우듬지 위에 살포시
올렸다 내렸다
꽃인 듯 임인 듯
가슴에 안기는 낮달.

# A Daytime Moon Hanging Over the Lake

Above Majang Lake
A first quarter moon that is fattening up
Slowly pulling it with my eyes
On an empty branch of a winter tree
Try to lift it precariously

Like seeing a beloved in a dream
With both eyes full of
Upon hanging it on the branch tip
Resembling the clear face of a lover
One flower is opening up

Catch it quietly with a gaze
Carefully on the treetop
Raising and lowering
As if it were a flower, as if it were a lover
The daytime moon comes embracing to the heart.

# 불도 추워 보인다

함박눈 내리는 밤
냉기 서린 옷자락 걸치고
화단에 외롭게 앉아 있는
나지막한 가로등 하나

매서운 바람은
웃음마저 얼리는데
가로등은 말없이
밤을 어루만지고 있다

깊어지는 고독이
밤의 적막을 채우고
따스한 온기 간절한 밤
하염없이 눈만 내린다

꽁꽁 언 내 마음
눈치라도 챈 걸까
오늘따라
불도 추워 보인다.

# Even the Fire Looks Cold

On a night of heavy snowfall
Clad in a hem laced with chill
Sitting lonely in a flower bed
A single low streetlamp

The bitter wind
Freezes even laughter
The streetlight silently
Soothes the night

Deepening solitude
Fills the silence of the night
A night longing for warmth
Endlessly, only snow falls

My frozen heart
Perhaps noticing
Today more than ever
Even the fire looks cold.

## 로스팅

생두를 세게 볶을수록
달콤한 향은 옅어지고
커피에 쓴맛만 커지듯

사랑도 세게 볶을수록
달콤한 마음은 옅어지고
쓰디쓴 상처만 커진다

생두이든 사랑이든
최상의 맛을 보려면
로스팅은 딱 거기까지만.

# Roasting

The harder you roast the green coffee beans, the more
Sweet scents fade away
As if the bitter taste only gets bigger in coffee

The more you stir-fry your love
Sweet heart becomes lighte
Only the bitter wound grows

Whether it's green beans or love
To get the best taste
Let's stop roasting there.

# 오리와 오리배

뭉게구름이 손잡고
드넓은 호수에
풍덩 빠져 놀고 있는데

어느샌가 오리 다가와
살랑살랑 파문이 일고
구름이 화들짝 놀란다

호숫가 오리 한 마리
물 위에선 유유자적
물 아래 발길질 바쁘고

호수 가운데 오리배는
사랑 싣고 두둥실
연인들 발길질 바쁘다.

## Duck and the Duck Boat

Cumulus clouds holding hands
Diving into the vast lake
Splashing around and playing

Before you know it, a duck approached
The lake is to rippling
The cloud was surprised

The duck on the surface of the lake
Looks comfortable on the water and
Kicking his feet busily under the water

Duck boat in the middle of the lake
Floats with love on board
Lovers keep their feet busy.

## 연지에서

한여름 진흙탕 연못에
그윽한 향기 채우고
세상 밝히는 연꽃

티 없이 고고한 얼굴
유연한 그 모습
평화롭고 아름답다

진흙탕에서도 꿋꿋이
피는 꽃, 지는 꽃
열매 맺는 씨방

그게 어디 꽃뿐이랴.

## In the Lotus Field

In a muddy pond in midsummer
Full of deep scent
A world-clearing lotus flower

A flawless and noble face
That flexible figure
Peaceful and beautiful

Steadfast even in the mud
Blooming flowers, falling flowers
Fruit-bearing lotus ovary

It's not just lotus flowers that do this.

# 생강나무 꽃

때 이른 봄
비밀스러운 몸짓으로
살금살금 제일 먼저 달려와
깊은 산길에 점점이 금가루 뿌리며
수줍은 고백 울컥 토해내니
가슴 속 깊이 담아 둔 더운 바람
속절없이 툭툭 불꽃처럼 터지네.

## Ginger Tree Flower

Early spring
With secretive gestures
Stealthily arriving first
Sprinkling gold dust in spots along the deep mountain trail
Since a shy confession is being blurted out
The warm wind held deep within my heart
Helplessly bursts out like sparks.

제 5 부

# 가을 숲에 서면

Part Ⅴ

# When I Stand in the Autumn Forest

# 겨울 호수

하얀 눈 소복한 상류에
고요 속에 잠긴 호수가
그대의 따뜻한 품처럼
하얀 숨결로 다가오고

끝없이 펼쳐진 호수는
얼음 녹은 물줄기 따라
파란 숨결 머금고
낯선 고독을 품고 있다

잔잔한 호수
반짝이는 윤슬은
차마 얼지 못한 내 마음
조용히 흔들어 깨우고

겨울 호수는 그렇게
멈춘 듯 흘러가며
봄날의 조각들
하나하나 꿰매고 있다.

## Winter Lake

In the white snow-covered upstream
A lake submerged in silence
Like your warm embrace
Comes with white breath

The endless lake
Following the stream of melted ice
With a blue breath
Have an unfamiliar solitude

Calm lake
The sparkling Yunseul
My heart that couldn't be frozen
Quietly shake me to wake me up

The winter lake is like that
It flows as if it has stopped
Pieces of spring Day
Stitching up that one by one.

# 한 해를 보내면서

연둣빛 속삭임을 시작으로
한여름 뙤약볕 숨결을 지나
단풍 노래하는 가을 숲길을 걸어
함박눈 내린 겨울 품에 이르기까지

사계절 소풍 길에서
꽃구경도 하고 돌부리도 만나고
세월의 강물 따라
부지런히 달려 여기까지 왔다

단 한 번뿐인 삶의 무대
지휘자도 연주자도 오롯이 내 몫인데
어설픈 화음도 빛나는 선율도
모두 내 손으로 그려가야 할 터

이제 한 해의 끝자락에 서서
새해 삶을 그려 갈 빈 도화지 펼친다
희망의 색으로 사랑의 선으로
곱게 채워 갈 또 다른 내일을 꿈꾸며.

## As the Year Draws to a Close

Starting with the whispers of spring in tender green
Passing through the breath of midsummer’s scorching sun
Walking the autumn forest path where maple leaves sing
Until I reach winter’s arms, wrapped in falling snow

On this picnic-like journey through four seasons
I admired flowers and stumbled upon stones
Following the river of time
I came all this way on a diligent run

On the stage of life that comes but once
Where I am both the conductor and performer
Even clumsy harmonies, even radiant melodies
I must draw them all with my own hands

Now, standing at the year's end
I unfold a blank canvas for the new year to come
With the color of hope, with the line of love
Dreaming of another tomorrow that will be filled beautifully.

# 가을 숲에 서면

색색 물감 풀어
숲마다 곱디고운
수채화 그려놓고

내 마음 온도
점점 달콤해져
하릴없이 나댄다

발아래 사각사각
자연이 연주하는
최고의 감성 악기

가을이다
암만 봐도 참 곱다
언제나 너처럼.

## When I Stand in the Autumn Forest

Release the colorful paints
Every forest is beautiful color
Have drawn a watercolor

My heart temperature
It's getting sweeter
My heart is fluttering uncontrollably

The sound of leaves crunching beneath my feet
Nature plays
It is the best emotional instrument

It's autumn
It's so beautiful to look at
At all times like you.

# 꿈

눈에 보이지 않아
날마다 마음으로 만지고

잡힐 듯 말 듯
애타게 밀고 당기며

넌 아직도
문밖에 서성이지만

나의 바다에
섬 하나 들여놓고

너를 맞으려
날마다 등불 밝힌다.

## Dream

Because it is invisible
I touch it with my heart every day

Caught, but not really
In a desperate push and pull

You're still
You're hovering outside the door, though

In my sea
I have made an island

To meet you
I leave the lamp on every day.

## 인연의 끈

만나야 할 인연은
먼 길 돌고 돌아서도
끝내 만나더라

정말 그렇더라
인연의 힘은
장벽도 소용없더라

한 줄기 지나가는
그냥 그런
바람인 줄 알았는데

그대 고운 이름으로
내 영혼 울창한 숲에
자분자분 들어와

오색실 한 땀 한 땀
정성 다해
튼실하게 수 놓더라

인연은
가시덤불에 걸어놔도
끝내 꽃 피우더라.

## String of Fate

Destiny we must meet
Even if I come back after a long way
Finally we meet each other

It was really like that
The power of fate
Any obstacle doesn't matter

A ray passing by
Just like that
I thought it was the wind

In your beautiful name
Into the dense forest of my soul
Came in little by little

One stitch of five-colored thread at a time
With all one's heart
Embroidered it sturdily

The fate is
Even if it is hung on the thorn bush
In the end, it blooms.

## 늦가을 그리고 밤

한낮의 소란스러운 터널을 지나
찬바람 어스름이 깔린 늦가을
달빛마저 오슬오슬 떨고 있는 밤

생각의 잔가지들 하나둘 잠재우고
오롯이 내가 나를 만나는
사유의 시간 고요가 참 좋다

어둠의 정적 깨고 귀뚜라미
계절 끝자락에서
마지막 콘서트 마무리 중이고

긴 적막의 밤을 지나
길섶 풀벌레들 옹알이로
새벽을 흔들어 깨우고 있다.

## Late Autumn and Night

Passing through a noisy tunnel in the middle of the day
Late fall, dark and cold windy
A night where even the moonlight trembles

Putting the twigs of thoughts to sleep one by one
It's only me who meets myself
I really like the quiet time of thinking

Crickets break the silence of darkness
At the end of the season
The last concert is wrapping up

After a long night of silence
The chirping of insects by the roadside
Shaking the dawn awake.

# 겨울 바닷가

겨울 동해 바닷가
찬바람이 날 세워
훅 찌르고 달아난다

그대와 거닐던
이 바닷가 파도
오늘 유독 쓸쓸하다

잠시의 시간 어느새
수많은 결로 흘러
그댈 아득히 잊은 줄 알았는데

한 발 두 발 걷다 보니
가는 곳마다
추억이 발길에 차인다.

## Winter Beach

Winter east sea beach
The cold wind sharpens its edge
Stabs me quickly and runs away

The sea I walked with you
The waves of this beach
Look particularly lonely today

A brief moment of time
Somehow flowed through countless seasons
I thought I had long forgotten you

As I walked one step, two steps
Everywhere I go
Memories are kicked by my footsteps.

# 비와 그대

그대는 참으로
놀라운 재주가 있네
내가 머무는 곳
주소도 모르면서

여름날 소낙비
장대 빗속을 뚫고
내 맘속에
쏜살같이 달려오네.

# Rain and You

You're really
You have amazing talent
Where I stay
You don't even know the address

Summer day shower
Through the heavy rain
Into my heart
It comes very quickly.

# 눈길 걸으며

선명한 발자국 뒤로
지나온 기억 저편에
아득히 멀어져가는
희미한 꿈의 조각들

차가운 바람 사이로
작은 온기 하나 스며들고
긴 겨울 끝자락에서
다시 꿈은 숨을 고른다

눈꽃 핀 가지 끝
움트는 봄의 숨결 따라
가만가만 꿈틀대는
연둣빛 꿈 하나

눈꽃 송이 모두 녹아내린
포근한 어느 날
봄이 말을 걸어오면
나는 그 꿈을 꼭 안아주리라.

## Walking on a Snowy Path

Behind clear footprints
Beyond the memories that have passed
Fade far away
Fragments of faint dreams

Through the cold wind
A small warmth seeps
At the trailing edge of a long winter
Once more, a dream gathers its breath

At the tip of a snow-blossomed branch
Following the budding breath of spring
Quietly, gently wriggling
One light green dream

All the snowflakes have melted away
One cozy day
When spring speaks to me
I will embrace that dream tightly.

# 십이월 문턱에서

길 떠나는 가을이
아무리 싫다 해도
나이에 보태라며

더해진 숫자 하나
슬며시 밀어주고
저만치 달아나네

천천히 떠나라고
아무리 꼬드겨도
잰걸음에 가버리네.

## On the Threshold of December

The autumn that is leaving
No matter how much I say I hate it
While saying to add to my age

One added number
Push it quietly and leave it
Fleeing far away

As I tell you to leave slowly
No matter how much I cajole
Runs away quickly.

제 6 부

# 그래 봄이야

Part Ⅵ

# So, It's Spring

# 그래 봄이야

보드란 바람결에
괜스레 설레는 맘

언 땅속 웅크렸던 꿈
하나둘 꿈틀거리네

겨우내 언 가슴
시나브로 풀리고

그래 이젠 봄이야
희망의 꽃대 오르는.

## So, It's Spring

In the gentle breeze
I feel excited for no reason

A dream curled up in the frozen ground
One by one, it's wiggling

A Frozen heart throughout the winter
It gradually loosens without being noticed

So it's spring now
Climbing the flower stalk of hope.

# 산다는 건

겨울 한파 몰아쳐
온 가슴 꽁꽁 얼어
죽을 것만 같았는데

내 안에 단비 내려
새순 돋아나는
연둣빛 봄이 오네요

그래서 또 이렇게
숨 쉬고
한세상 사나 봐요.

## Living is

Winter cold wave hits
My whole heart is frozen solid
I felt like I was going to die

Sweet rain falls inside me
New shoots sprouting
Light green spring is coming

So again like this
While breathing
I guess we live for a lifetime.

# 사랑하는 일

시선 한곳에 두고
온 정성 다해
연 날리는 일이다

너무 풀면 사라지고
너무 세차게 당기면
줄이 뚝 끊어지고 마는

진실한 마음 담아
당겼다 풀었다
정성 다하는 일이다.

## To Love is

With one's eyes in one place
With all one's heart
It's like flying a kite

If you solve too much, it disappears
If you pull too hard
The line suddenly breaks

With a sincere heart
Pull and release
It's something you do with sincerity.

# 모닝커피

나의 하루를
가만히
열어 주는 열쇠

비 오나
눈 오나
바람 불어도

내 하루 출발선
정신 줄 잡아 주는
넌 나의 껌딱지.

## Morning Coffee

My day
Quietly
The key that opens

Even on rainy days
Even on snowy days
Even on windy days

The starting line of my day
Helps me stay focused
My an inseparable presence.

## 경계선

하늘 맞닿은 바다
눈으로 선 하나 그어
수평선이라 부르고

하늘 맞닿은 땅
눈으로 선 하나 그어
지평선이라 부르니

그대와 나 사이
마음으로 그은 선 하나
무슨 선이라 부를까

조금만 더 다가서면
모두 한순간에
허물어질 그 경계선.

## Borderline

The sea touching the sky
Draw a line with your eyes
It's called the horizontal line

Land that touches the sky
Draw a line with your eyes
It's called the horizon

Between you and me
A line drawn by heart
What line should I call it

Just a little closer
In a moment everyone
That borderline will crumble.

## 잠 못 드는 밤

밤 빗소리에
토닥토닥 자장가 삼아
잠 청해 보려는데

빗소리에 붙잡혀 온
오만가지 생각 줄기
끝도 없이 대롱대롱

이리 뒤척 저리 뒤척
생각 줄기 너를 잡고
밀고 당기다 보니

오늘도 어느새
부지런한 새벽이
기지개 켜고 일어나네.

# A Sleepless Night

To the sound of rain at night
Pat pat pat it as a lullaby
I'm trying to sleep

Caught by the sound of rain
Hundreds of thousands of thoughts
It hangs endlessly

Tossing and turning this and that
Grasping the stream of thoughts
As I kept pushing and pulling

Already today again
Diligent dawn
Wake up stretching.

# 그림자

본디 하나인 내가
가끔은 둘이 된다

햇살 눈 부신 날엔
더욱 신명 나게 졸졸
삼백예순다섯 날
좋다 싫다 내색 없는
또 하나의 나

도무지 뗄 수 없어
이 세상 끝까지 함께 할
우린 숙명적인 관계
미우나 고우나
내가 널 사랑할 수밖에.

## My Shadow

Originally it was one
But sometimes it becomes two

On a sunny day
Fllow me more
Three hundred and sixty-five days
Without saying that you like it or dislike it
Another me

Because we can't break up
We'll be together until the end of this world
We have a fateful relationship
When I hate you and when I like you
I can't help but love you.

## 호수

윤슬 반짝이는 호수
무시로 바람 불면
소리 없는 몸짓으로
가만가만 찰랑이고

드넓은 호숫가에
나 홀로 서서
분홍빛 연가
속으로 삼키는데

임 그리는 내 맘처럼
얼마나 깊고 깊은지
구름이 빠져 있고
하늘까지 빠져 있네.

## Lake

Yunseul sparkling lake
When the wind blows without warning
With a silent gesture
It is quietly rippling

On the shore of a wide lake
I stand alone
Pink love song
I swallow it inside

Like my heart yearning for you
How deep and deep the lake is
The clouds have fallen into the lake
And even the sky is submerged in the lake.

## 아메리카노

한 때는
커피잔에 달콤하게
설탕 넣었는데

살다 보니
입에 쓴 아메리카노
뗄 수 없는 친구네

달콤하든 쓰든
이젠 모두 아는 맛
바로 인생의 맛이네.

# Americano

At one time
Sweet in a coffee cup
I added sugar

As I live
A bitter Americano in mouth
It has become an inseparable friend

Sweet taste and bitter taste
The taste that everyone knows now
That's the taste of life.

# 내비게이션

쉽게 알 수 없는
미로 같은 길 뚫고
그대에게 가는 길

앗, 이런
잠깐 한눈팔아
경로 이탈했네

정신 줄 다시 잡고
재탐색해서
앞만 보고 달려가는

나의 최종 목적지
사랑하는
그대에게 가는 길.

## Navigation

Not easily known
Breaking through a maze-like path
The road to you

Oh my
I looked away for a moment and
I went off course

I came to my senses again
By searching again
Running only looking ahead

My final destination
Loving
The road to you.

문학세계대표작가선 1051

바다에서 별을 낚다

I Fished Up a Star from the Sea

류인순 한영시집

Ryu In-Soon's Korean-English Poetry Collection

인쇄 1판 1쇄 2025년 6월 17일
발행 1판 1쇄 2025년 6월 24일

지 은 이 : 류인순
펴 낸 이 : 김천우
펴 낸 곳 : 문학세계 출판부 / 도서출판 천우
등 록 : 1992. 2. 15. 제1-1307호
주 소 : 서울시 광진구 구의강변로 85 강우빌딩 7F
전 화 : 02)2298-7661
팩 스 : 02)2298-7665
http://cafe.naver.com/chunwu777
E-mail : cw7661@naver.com



값 25,000원



ISBN 978-89-7954-958-4